Cooking
with
Mickey
& Friends

Healthy Recipes from Your Favorite Disney Characters

Pat Baird

Disney PRESS

New York

Contents

A Word from Mickey

Hi, boys and girls!

Welcome to the kitchen. I bet you're surprised to see me here. Well, I'm not alone. All your other Disney pals are here, too. Most of the time you see us in all sorts of adventures. We run, jump, and play. We've all got lots of energy. That's because we like to eat, and we eat well. So we thought we would share some of our favorite recipes with you.

We picked recipes that everyone of all ages will like to eat. Sometimes you might see a recipe or an ingredient you haven't eaten before. Try it! Part of the fun of eating is tasting new food. The other part of eating is that it helps us to think better, grow taller and stronger, and even play better.

How do you know what to eat and how much? Think *variety*. This involves eating a few different foods from all the food groups every day.

Whole grain cereals, breads, and grains	**6 or more servings**
Vegetables	**3 or more servings**
Low-fat milk, cheese, yogurt, and other dairy products	**3 or more servings**
Lean meats, poultry (such as chicken and turkey), eggs, beans, nuts, or seeds	**2 servings**
Fruits	**2 or more servings**

The meat department of your local supermarket certainly offers a great deal of variety—so which are the lean ones? Lean meats don't have a thick layer of fat around the outside, or lots of white fatty streaks you can see. For ground meat (the kind you use for burgers or meat loaf), you need to read the label since the fat is mixed into the meat. Choose the packages

Simba says:

What's a serving?
Simple. Any one of these:

- *3/4 cup 100% pure fruit juice*
- *1 cup salad greens (go for the deep, dark green ones)*
- *1 medium fruit or vegetable*
- *1/2 cup fresh, frozen, or canned fruit or vegetable*
- *1/4 cup dried fruit (like raisins, apricots, and apples)*

marked "lean" or "extra lean." For poultry, a lean choice is the white meat instead of the dark.

Vegetables and fruits especially offer a great deal of variety. To make choosing easier, eat by color! When you're at the produce department, choose fruits and vegetables of different colors: green, red, orange, and white. Eating by color means you're getting lots of different vitamins and minerals, and other good stuff.

Another way to think of food is: *Every Day Foods* and *Sometimes Foods*. Along with fruits and vegetables, Every Day Foods include cereals and grains; milk, and other low-fat dairy products; and meat, poultry, and fish. Then foods like sugar, fat, desserts, and soda are Sometimes Foods. Have these once in a while—for fun!

Be smart about how much you eat, and how often you eat it. *Balance* is what we call it. For instance, if you have a burger, fries, and some ice cream for lunch, that meal has a lot of fat. So, for dinner, try a low-fat meal, such as spaghetti and tomato sauce, a salad, some fruit, and graham crackers.

From time to time in this book, I'll have a Nutri Tip for you, giving you some further tips on nutrition. Minnie, too, will offer some helpful advice in her Minnie Minders, such as ideas for how to do things faster and easier in the kitchen. In fact, everyone wanted to do more than just give a recipe or two. They insisted on providing you with some advice on eating. Mostly, though, we all want you to have fun. Cooking is a terrific way to do that.

So, what are you waiting for? Let's get cookin'!

Mickey Mouse

Minnie's Minders

Hi, kids!

Ready to get started? Good. Before you begin there are a few things to know:

❶ Read the recipe carefully. Make sure you have all the utensils and ingredients listed to make it.

❷ Set everything you'll need out on a countertop or a table. Measure all the ingredients and put them on a large tray.

❸ Reread the recipe to be sure you understand the steps. Double-check the utensils and ingredients.

❹ Ask an adult to help if you have questions, or if there's something like draining hot pasta or slicing to be done. This sign (Ask an Adult) will appear next to steps where adult supervision is needed. Always ask if there's anything you're unsure about. Be safe, not sorry.

❺ Tie back your hair if it's long. And, yes, all cooks wear aprons. Roll up your sleeves so they don't get dirty, caught on anything, or hang too close to a hot flame.

Remember: KEEP IT CLEAN. KEEP IT SAFE.

❶ Gather around the sink and wash your hands with warm, soapy water. (That goes for adult helpers, too!)

❷ Clean up spills and dribbles as you go along. That will help you avoid accidents and extra work later.

❸ Keep a damp sponge or some paper towels handy.

❹ Keep thick, dry oven mitts or pot holders nearby. They help prevent burns. Wet ones cause burns because the heat goes right through.

❺ Turn the handles of saucepans and skillets away from you and toward the middle of the stove when cooking. That keeps them from catching on something (or someone), or getting knocked over.

❻ When you've finished, put knives and other sharp objects aside and ask an adult to wash them separately. Then get to work washing and drying the other dishes and utensils, or load them into the dishwasher. Put away any utensils and foods you've used.

❼ Wash your hands again. Take off your apron and put it in the laundry.

❽ Remember to recycle. Separate the cans, foil, glass, and plastic containers from the other trash when you're cleaning up.

Throughout, I'll be offering hints and suggestions to make things easier for you.

Now you're ready to begin!

Minnie Mouse

Breakfast

- ❖ Belle's Favorite Eggs

- ❖ Donald's Muffin Breakfast Sandwich

- ❖ Daisy's Muffin Breakfast Sandwich

- ❖ Goofy's Smart-Start Oatmeal

- ❖ Three Caballeros' Breakfast Burrito

- ❖ Mickey's Whole Wheat Honey Pancakes

- ❖ Cinderella's Pumpkin Waffles

Belle's Favorite Eggs

Serves 1

UTENSILS

- Small saucepan
- Oven mitt
- Spoon
- Cutting knife
- Cutting board
- Small bowl
- Fork
- Kitchen scissors OR knife
- 1 tablespoon measuring spoon
- 1/2 teaspoon measuring spoon

INGREDIENTS

- 2 eggs
- 1/2 slice low-fat ham
- 1 tablespoon low-fat mayonnaise
- 1/2 teaspoon mustard

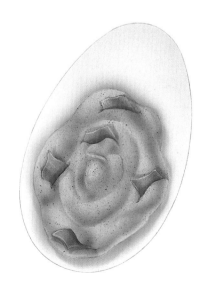

PLACE the eggs gently in saucepan. Cover with water, and bring to a boil over high heat. Turn heat to low, and simmer for 10 minutes.

 USE an oven mitt, and carefully take the pan off the heat. Place it in the sink, and pour out the water.

RUN cold water over the eggs in the pan. Let stand for 3 minutes.

CRACK the shells carefully with the back of a spoon. When the eggs are cool enough to handle, peel the eggs.

 CUT each of the eggs in half the long way to make 2 ovals.
Use a spoon to remove the yolks from the eggs.
Throw away one egg yolk. Place the other one in a small bowl.

 CUT the ham carefully into small pieces using the kitchen scissors OR knife. Place it in the bowl.

ADD the mayonnaise and mustard. Use a fork to mix them well.

SPOON the mixture into each of the egg halves.

Donald's Muffin Breakfast Sandwich

Serves 1

UTENSILS

- ❖ Toaster OR toaster oven
- ❖ Oven mitt
- ❖ Small plate
- ❖ 1 tablespoon measuring spoon
- ❖ 1 teaspoon measuring spoon
- ❖ Bread knife

INGREDIENTS

- ❖ 1 honey oat bran English muffin
- ❖ 1 tablespoon peanut butter
- ❖ 2 teaspoons honey OR jelly
- ❖ 1/2 small banana (peeled)

Mickey's Nutri Tip

Of course you can't eat cereal and milk in the car. But when I'm late, this is easy to wrap and eat along the way. Breakfast is my number one way to start the day.

Breakfast is the real power meal of the day. I energize with oatmeal, pancakes, frozen or homemade waffles, whole grain cereal and milk, or a bagel and juice. You don't feel much like eating in the morning? That's okay. Shake up a quick boost made with low-fat milk or yogurt and your favorite fruit. Or, you can whirl it in a blender. Whatever you choose, breakfast is the heroic way to start the day.

SPLIT the English muffin gently in half. Toast until golden brown. Use an oven mitt and carefully remove it from the toaster.

PLACE half the muffin on a small plate. Spread the peanut butter on top.

SPREAD the honey OR jelly on the other half.

SLICE the banana carefully in half and place it on top of the honey OR jelly. Cover with the other half of the English muffin.

 CUT the sandwich in half, if desired.

Daisy's Muffin Breakfast Sandwich

Serves 1

UTENSILS

- ❖ Can opener (if using canned pineapple)
- ❖ Fork
- ❖ 1 paper towel folded in half 2 times to make a square
- ❖ Toaster OR toaster oven
- ❖ Oven mitt
- ❖ 1 tablespoon measuring spoon
- ❖ 1/4 teaspoon measuring spoon
- ❖ Bread knife

INGREDIENTS

- ❖ 1 whole pineapple ring (canned OR fresh*)
- ❖ 1 honey wheat English muffin
- ❖ 2 tablespoons low-fat cottage cheese OR low-fat cream cheese
- ❖ 1/4 teaspoon ground cinnamon
- ❖ 1/4 teaspoon sugar

*Look in the produce section of the supermarket for pineapples that are already peeled and cored. They're sold in a plastic bag.

Be sure to check the setting on your toaster or toaster oven. Make sure it's on LIGHT. If the English muffin is too dark and crisp, it will be tricky to cut.

A bread knife has a serrated (bumpy) edge. That makes it easier to cut the bread without tearing it.

OPEN the can of pineapple rings if you don't have fresh pineapple. Use a fork to take out one of the rings and place it on a folded paper towel to drain.

SPLIT the English muffin gently in half, and toast lightly. Carefully remove with an oven mitt.

SPREAD the cottage cheese OR cream cheese on one half of the muffin. Place the pineapple ring on top.

SPRINKLE the cinnamon and sugar evenly over the pineapple. Place the other half of the muffin on top.

 CUT the sandwich in half.

(15)

Mickey's Nutri Tip

Look at this! Cottage cheese in a sandwich. What a good way to get protein and calcium! For a super boost, have a glass of milk, too.

Goofy's Smart-Start Oatmeal

Serves 1

UTENSILS

❖ Small saucepan and cover

❖ 1 cup liquid measuring cup

❖ 1/4 cup dry measuring cup

❖ 1 tablespoon measuring spoon

❖ Spoon

❖ Oven mitt

❖ Small bowl

❖ 1 teaspoon measuring spoon

INGREDIENTS

❖ 1/2 cup water

❖ 1/4 cup old-fashioned oatmeal

❖ Pinch of salt

❖ 1/4 cup unsweetened chunky applesauce

❖ 2 tablespoons instant non-fat dry milk

❖ 1 tablespoon raisins

❖ Pinch of ground cinnamon

❖ 1 teaspoon sugar

❖ 1/3 cup low-fat milk

Doc says:

That fiber stuff everybody's talking about is important for kids, too. It's only found in plant and vegetable food. The funny part is fiber isn't really digested. But it helps move food through the body. Everybody should eat fruits, vegetables, whole grain cereals, and bread for fiber each day.

BRING the water to a boil in a small saucepan. Add the oatmeal and salt. Reduce the heat to low. Cook for 5 minutes, stirring occasionally.

 **USE** an oven mitt, and remove the pan from heat. Stir in the applesauce and dry milk. Add the raisins and cinnamon. Stir again and cover the pan. Let stand for 3 minutes.

SPOON the oatmeal into a small bowl to serve. Sprinkle with sugar, and pour the milk over the top.

17

Three Caballeros' Breakfast Burrito

Serves 1

UTENSILS

- ❖ Small microwave-safe bowl
- ❖ 1 tablespoon measuring spoon
- ❖ 2 forks
- ❖ Oven mitt
- ❖ 3 paper towels
- ❖ Microwave-safe plate OR paper plate

INGREDIENTS

- ❖ 1 egg
- ❖ 1 egg white
- ❖ 1 tablespoon milk OR water
- ❖ One 10-inch whole wheat OR flour tortilla
- ❖ 2 tablespoons shredded low-fat cheese, any kind
- ❖ 2 tablespoons mild salsa

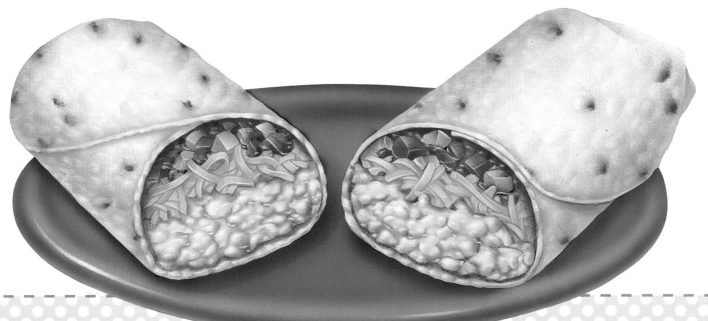

COMBINE the egg, egg white, and milk OR water in a small microwave-safe bowl. Stir with a fork until blended.

MICROWAVE on HIGH for 30 seconds. Stir well with a fork. Microwave on HIGH again for 20 seconds. Stir again, and microwave once more for about 15 seconds, or until the eggs are cooked.

REMOVE the bowl from the microwave with an oven mitt. Cover the bowl with a paper towel.

PLACE the tortilla between two paper towels, and put it on a microwave-safe plate OR paper plate. Microwave on HIGH for 10 seconds. Use an oven mitt to remove from the microwave. Throw away the top paper towel.

SPOON the scrambled eggs onto the center of the flour tortilla. Use the side of a clean fork to spread the eggs, leaving a one-inch border on all sides. Sprinkle the cheese on top. Spoon the salsa on top of the cheese.

FOLD UP the bottom edge of the tortilla. Then fold the right edge over to just cover the eggs, and bring the left edge over that to make a burrito.

WRAP a napkin or paper towel around the bottom half, and eat the burrito as a sandwich.

Mickey's Whole Wheat Honey Pancakes

Makes twelve 3-inch pancakes

UTENSILS

- ❖ Medium mixing bowl
- ❖ Small mixing bowl
- ❖ 1/2 cup dry measuring cup
- ❖ 1/4 cup dry measuring cup
- ❖ 1/2 teaspoon measuring spoon
- ❖ 1/4 teaspoon measuring spoon
- ❖ 2 mixing spoons
- ❖ 1 cup liquid measuring cup
- ❖ 1 tablespoon measuring spoon
- ❖ Large skillet OR pancake griddle

INGREDIENTS

- ❖ 1/2 cup all-purpose flour
- ❖ 1/4 cup whole wheat flour
- ❖ 1/4 cup toasted wheat germ
- ❖ 1/2 teaspoon baking powder
- ❖ 1/2 teaspoon baking soda
- ❖ 1/4 teaspoon salt
- ❖ 1 egg
- ❖ 1 cup low-fat milk
- ❖ 2 tablespoons vegetable oil
- ❖ 2 tablespoons honey
- ❖ Nonstick cooking spray

COMBINE the flours, wheat germ, baking powder, baking soda, and salt in a medium bowl. Stir to mix it well.

COMBINE the egg, milk, oil, and honey in a small bowl. Stir to mix it well.

POUR the egg mixture into the flour mixture. Stir it gently until it is a smooth batter.

HEAT a large skillet OR pancake griddle over medium-high heat. Spray it lightly with cooking oil.

USE a 1/4 cup measuring cup—not completely full—to pour the batter onto the skillet or griddle. Cook the pancakes for about 3 minutes, or until little bubbles appear on top. Turn the pancakes over, and cook 1 to 2 minutes longer, until they're golden brown.

21

Mickey's Nutri Tip

What makes these pancakes special is the added wheat germ. It has a sweet, nutty taste. Wheat germ is a good source of vitamin E and fiber. Add it to cereal, ice cream, or yogurt for a crunchy treat.

Cinderella's Pumpkin Waffles

*Makes four 7-inch waffles**

UTENSILS

- ❖ Waffle maker
- ❖ Large mixing bowl
- ❖ 1 cup dry measuring cup
- ❖ 1/2 cup dry measuring cup
- ❖ 1/4 cup dry measuring cup
- ❖ 1 teaspoon measuring spoon
- ❖ Small mixing bowl
- ❖ 1 cup liquid measuring cup
- ❖ 1 tablespoon measuring spoon
- ❖ 1 whisk OR 2 mixing spoons
- ❖ Soup spoon
- ❖ Fork
- ❖ Oven mitt

*Waffle makers come in different sizes. You may have to adjust this recipe to suit the one you have at home.

INGREDIENTS

- ❖ 1 1/2 cups all-purpose flour
- ❖ 1/4 cup packed dark brown sugar
- ❖ 2 teaspoons baking powder
- ❖ 1 teaspoon ground cinnamon
- ❖ 1 teaspoon salt
- ❖ 1 egg
- ❖ 1 1/4 cups low-fat milk
- ❖ 1/2 cup canned pumpkin (not pumpkin pie mix)
- ❖ 2 tablespoons vegetable oil
- ❖ Nonstick cooking spray

PREHEAT the waffle maker according to its directions.

COMBINE the flour, sugar, baking powder, cinnamon, and salt in a large bowl. Lightly whisk, or stir, to mix it well. You may need to crumble any bits of brown sugar with your fingers to be sure there are no lumps. Then whisk it again.

It's nice to keep the cooked waffles warm while you make the others. A 200°F oven will help. The waffles can be put on the oven rack or on a plate in a single layer. Be sure to ask for help here. Use oven mitt when removing them from the oven.

COMBINE the egg, milk, pumpkin, and oil in a small bowl. Whisk, or stir, to mix them well.

POUR the egg mixture into the flour mixture. Stir it gently until it forms a smooth batter.

SPRAY both sides of the waffle maker lightly with nonstick cooking spray.

USE a 1/2 cup measuring cup to pour a heaping amount of the batter onto the grids. Scrape out the inside of the cup with a soup spoon (this is a fairly thick batter). Use the spoon to spread the batter to the edges of the grids. Close the top, and cook for about 4 minutes (some waffle makers have a light that tells you when they're done), or until the waffle is set and the top opens easily. Use a fork to remove the waffle.

Lunch

- ❖ Aladdin's Magic Carpet Rolls

- ❖ Chef Louis's Clam Chowder

- ❖ Goofy's Easy as A-B-C Soup

- ❖ Pumbaa's "Slimy Yet Satisfying" Chicken Noodle Soup

- ❖ Mickey's Neato Burrito

Aladdin's Magic Carpet Rolls

Serves 1

UTENSILS

❖ Cutting knife

❖ Cutting board

❖ Toothpicks

❖ Small dish

INGREDIENTS

❖ 2 slices soft whole wheat OR white bread

❖ 2 slices low-fat cooked ham

❖ 2 slices low-fat American OR Swiss cheese

❖ Mustard (for dipping)

PLACE the bread on a cutting board.

CUT the crusts off both slices of bread.

PLACE 1 slice of ham and 1 slice of cheese on top of each slice of bread.

STARTING at one end, carefully roll up the bread, ham, and cheese, forming a long roll.

PUT a toothpick in the middle to hold it together.

MAKE another roll, using the other slice of bread, ham, and cheese.

SERVE the rolls with a small dish of mustard for dipping.

Mickey's Nutri Tip

Sometimes I use turkey or roast beef to make this. They're good protein foods, and the cheese gives me calcium. I have Peter Pan's Sparkling Pink Punch (page 72) to drink.

Chef Louis's Clam Chowder

Serves 4 (1 3/4 cups each)

UTENSILS

❖ Can opener

❖ Strainer

❖ Small bowl

❖ Cutting board

❖ Chopping knife

❖ Potato peeler

❖ 1 teaspoon measuring spoon

❖ 3-quart saucepan and cover

❖ 1 cup liquid measuring cup

❖ 1 large stirring spoon

❖ Ladle

❖ 4 small soup bowls

INGREDIENTS

❖ Two 6 1/2-ounce cans minced clams packed in clam juice

❖ 1 small onion

❖ 2 medium potatoes

❖ 1 teaspoon vegetable oil

❖ One 8-ounce bottle clam juice

❖ 3 cups low-fat milk

❖ Salt and pepper to taste

28

OPEN the clams and drain the juice into a small bowl. Set the clams and the juice aside.

 PEEL the onion, using a knife, and cut it into small pieces. (You should have about 1/2 cup.) Set aside.

 USE the peeler to peel the potatoes. Cut them into 1/2-inch cubes. Set aside.

 HEAT the oil in the saucepan over medium-low heat for 1 minute. Add the onion, and cook for 2 minutes, stirring frequently.

ADD the potatoes, the juice from the clams, and the bottle of clam juice. Stir well.

COVER the pot partially, and cook over medium heat for 15 minutes, stirring occasionally.

REDUCE the heat to low. Add the strained clams. Slowly pour in the milk, stirring constantly.

RE-COVER the pot partially, cook for 10 minutes longer. Add salt and pepper to taste.

 LADLE the soup carefully into bowls and serve.

Aladdin says:

Be adventurous. Try new foods. I've tried Chinese noodles, Italian chicken, and different kinds of melon. Start with just one bite. Who knows? Maybe you'll discover a new favorite.

Mickey's Nutri Tip

No doubt about it, I want to keep my bones strong and healthy. So I go for the calcium whenever I can. I like the way Chef Louis uses milk in this yummy soup.

Goofy's Easy as A-B-c Vegetable Soup

Serves 4 (1 1/2 cups each)

UTENSILS

- ❖ Can opener
- ❖ 3-quart saucepan and cover
- ❖ 1/4 teaspoon measuring spoon
- ❖ 1 cup dry measuring cup
- ❖ 1/2 cup dry measuring cup
- ❖ Kitchen scissors
- ❖ Ladle
- ❖ 4 small soup bowls

INGREDIENTS

- ❖ Two 13 3/4-ounce cans reduced-sodium chicken broth
- ❖ One 10-ounce package frozen mixed vegetables
- ❖ 1/4 teaspoon onion powder
- ❖ 1 cup canned drained cannellini beans (or your favorite type of canned beans)
- ❖ 1/2 cup alphabet macaroni (see Minnie Minder)
- ❖ 2 sprigs fresh parsley
- ❖ Grated Romano OR Parmesan cheese (optional)

Mickey's Nutri Tip

Good deal! Vegetables and beans are two of my favorite foods because they both have fiber. Beans are a bonus because they have protein, too. The macaroni is f-u-n, as Goofy would say.

OPEN the cans of chicken broth and pour into the saucepan. Add the vegetables and onion powder.

COVER and bring to a boil over high heat. Reduce the heat to medium. Cook for 5 minutes longer.

STIR in the beans and macaroni, and re-cover. Cook for about 10 minutes, or until the macaroni is tender, stirring occasionally.

TURN OFF the heat. Snip the parsley into small pieces with kitchen scissors and add to the soup.

LADLE the soup into bowls. Sprinkle with grated cheese, if desired.

Minnie Minder

When I make this, I sometimes use other shapes of small macaroni. Little elbows or shells are nice. You can also find shapes like hearts, dinosaurs, and autumn leaves that come in colors, too!

31

Pumbaa's "Slimy Yet Satisfying" Chicken Noodle Soup

Serves 2 (about 1 1/2 cups each)

UTENSILS

❖ 2-quart saucepan

❖ 1 cup liquid measuring cup

❖ Can opener

❖ Medium bowl

❖ Fork

❖ Strainer

❖ Ladle

❖ 2 small soup bowls

INGREDIENTS

❖ 1 1/2 ounces bean thread noodles (see Minnie Minder)

❖ 2 cups warm water

❖ One 5-ounce can chunk white chicken, packed in water

❖ One 13 3/4-ounce can reduced-sodium chicken broth

❖ 3/4 cup water

PLACE the noodles in the saucepan, and cover with 2 cups *warm* water. Let soak (don't cook) for 10 minutes.

OPEN AND empty the can of chicken, and any juice, into a medium bowl. Use a fork to mash into small pieces. Set aside.

USE a fork to stir the noodles, when 10 minutes are up. Use a strainer to drain the noodles over the sink.

OPEN and pour the chicken broth and water into the saucepan. Bring to a boil over high heat.

ADD the noodles and the chicken. Reduce the heat to medium. Cook for 10 minutes longer.

LADLE the soup carefully into bowls and serve.

You might need a fork to eat this soup. The bean-thread noodles are very slippery. That makes them tricky to eat. Look for them in the Oriental food section of your supermarket. They are also called Sai Fun, *or cellophane noodles. Usually there are three "bundles" of noodles in a 3 3/4-ounce package. Use one of the bundles to make the soup. Angel hair pasta or cappellini can be used, too. Don't soak the pasta, just add it with the chicken.*

33

Mickey's Neato Burrito

Serves 2 to 4

UTENSILS

- ❖ Fork
- ❖ Medium mixing bowl
- ❖ 1 cup dry measuring cup
- ❖ 1/2 cup dry measuring cup
- ❖ 1 microwave-safe plate
- ❖ Paper towel
- ❖ Oven mitt
- ❖ Small spatula

INGREDIENTS

- ❖ 3/4 cup low-fat refried beans
- ❖ 1/2 cup low-fat shredded cheddar cheese
- ❖ 1/2 cup mild salsa
- ❖ Four 6-inch whole wheat OR flour tortillas

All you vegetarians will like this recipe. Beans, cheese, and tortillas (bread) are good foods to eat together.

USE a fork to combine the beans, cheese, and salsa in a medium bowl. Mix them well.

PLACE 1 tortilla on the counter. Loosely fill a 1/2 cup dry measuring cup with the bean mixture. Place mixture in the middle of the tortilla. Use a fork to form a line about 2 inches wide down the center. Leave about 1 inch at the top and bottom.

FOLD UP about 1 inch on the bottom of the tortilla to keep the filling in. Bring the folded bottom edge up to the center and then bring the top edge down to close. Tuck the open ends under.

PLACE the tortilla roll on the plate with the tucked sides down.

REPEAT with the other 3 tortillas. Place them on the plate so they look like the spokes of a wheel.

MICROWAVE on HIGH for 45 seconds. Use oven mitt to remove the plate from the microwave. Let stand for 1 minute. Use a small spatula to serve the burritos.

35

Minnie Minder

It's very important to wait a minute (or two) when you take food out of a microwave. Because it cooks so fast it needs time to finish getting done. Be careful when you take a bite. The food can be hotter than you think.

Smart microwave cooks use a few seconds less—not more—when cooking to avoid burns, overcooking, and possibly spoiling a recipe.

Snacks & Side Dishes

- ❖ The Sultan's Hummus Dip with Veggies

- ❖ Abu's Baked Apples

- ❖ Rafiki's Coconut Fruit Kabobs

- ❖ Dumbo's Broccoli Slaw

- ❖ Thumper's Buttered Baby Carrots

- ❖ Alice's Cheesy Rice

- ❖ Pocahontas's Triple Corn Bread

The Sultan's Hummus Dip with Fresh Vegetables

Serves 3 to 4 (Makes 1 1/2 cups)

UTENSILS

❖ Can opener

❖ Strainer

❖ Food processor OR blender

❖ 1 tablespoon measuring spoon

❖ 1/4 teaspoon measuring spoon

❖ Rubber scraper OR spoon

❖ Small bowl

❖ Medium plate

INGREDIENTS

❖ One 15-ounce can chickpeas (garbanzo beans)

❖ Juice of 1/2 lemon (about 2 tablespoons)

❖ 1/4 teaspoon garlic powder

❖ 3 sprigs fresh parsley

❖ 1/4 cup low-fat plain yogurt

FOR DIPPING

An assortment of any fresh vegetables: carrot sticks, celery sticks, green or red pepper slices, cucumber slices; or triangles of whole wheat pita bread

Mickey's Nutri Tip

This is so good I sometimes have it for lunch or dinner. You can, too. Just spoon some of the hummus into a pita pocket. Then put in some veggies. Have it with a glass of milk. Wow! A complete meal in a pocket!

Here's a chance to go to the grocery salad bar. Pick your favorite vegetables. Everything is already washed and sliced for you.

Remember to play it safe when using a food processor or blender. Handle the blades carefully, or ask for help. Make sure the lid is in place before turning on the motor. Always unplug the machine before opening the lid or removing the container from the base.

OPEN the can of chickpeas, and use the strainer to drain out the liquid over the sink.

COMBINE the chickpeas, lemon juice, garlic powder, parsley, and yogurt in the workbowl of a food processor (or the container of a blender). Lock the top, or put the lid firmly in place.

Ask an Adult **PUREE** until smooth. Once or twice, turn off the machine and scrape the sides of the workbowl or container.

SPOON the hummus mixture into a small bowl.

PLACE the fresh vegetables, or pita triangles, on a plate. Dip into the hummus and enjoy!

39

Abu's Baked Apples

Serves 2

UTENSILS

- Plastic apple corer (see Minnie Minder)
- Small microwave-safe baking dish
- 1/4 cup dry measuring cup
- 1/2 teaspoon measuring spoon
- Plastic wrap
- Oven mitt
- Serving spoon

INGREDIENTS

- 2 large apples
- 1/4 cup apple juice OR apple cider
- 1/4 cup maple syrup
- 1/2 teaspoon ground cinnamon

40

Bambi says:

Think you get vitamin C just from eating oranges or drinking juice? Well, look at the lineup. Tomatoes, green peppers, pineapples, peaches, cantaloupes, and tangerines are some of the vitamin-C-rich foods to try. Kiwi, raspberries, strawberries, spinach, and potatoes are other good choices, too. Have at least one serving every day.

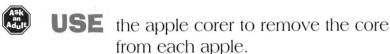 **USE** the apple corer to remove the core from each apple.

PLACE the apples in a small microwave-safe dish.

POUR the apple juice and maple syrup over the apples and sprinkle the cinnamon on top.

COVER the baking dish loosely with plastic wrap.

PLACE the baking dish in the microwave. Cook the apples on HIGH for about 4 minutes. (If your microwave doesn't have a rotating bottom, turn the dish a 1/2 turn after 2 minutes. Then cook for 2 minutes longer.)

 **USE** oven mitt to remove the dish from the microwave. Let stand (covered) for 3 minutes before serving. Carefully remove the plastic wrap.

PLACE an apple in a small dish, and spoon some of the cooking syrup over the top.

41

Minnie Minder

You can buy a plastic apple corer that is easy to use. It's safer than a knife.

When removing plastic wrap from cooked foods, start from the side of the dish furthest from you and peel it back. Turn your head to the side in case there is still any steam under the wrap. If you peel the apples before cooking, reduce the time to 2 1/2 minutes.

Mickey's Nutri Tip

I always eat apples with the skin on. That way I get extra fiber. Sometimes for variation I cut the cooked apple into little pieces. I put them in a bowl and stir in yogurt and granola with some of the cooking syrup mixed in.

Rafiki's Coconut Fruit Kabobs

Serves 2

UTENSILS

❖ Can opener

❖ Medium bowl

❖ Chopping knife

❖ Cutting board

❖ Plastic apple corer
(See page 43)

❖ Large spoon

❖ 4 small wooden skewers
(about 6 inches long)

❖ 1 medium plate

❖ 1/4 cup dry measuring cup

INGREDIENTS

❖ One 8-ounce can pineapple
chunks, packed in juice

❖ 1 medium banana, peeled

❖ 1 medium apple

❖ 1/4 cup orange juice

❖ 1/4 cup shredded coconut

You can cover these kabobs with plastic wrap and put them in the refrigerator. Then your snack is ready when you are. Eat these kabobs within 24 hours.

OPEN the can of pineapple chunks. Pour the pineapple chunks and juice into a medium bowl.

 SLICE the banana into 1-inch pieces. Add to the bowl.

USE apple corer to remove the core from the apple. Cut the apple into 1-inch cubes. Add to the bowl.

POUR the orange juice over the fruit and stir to blend.

PUT the fruit on a skewer, alternating the chunks of pineapple, banana, and apple. Fill up each skewer with an equal amount of fruit.

POUR half the coconut onto a plate. Place the skewers on top. Sprinkle remaining coconut over the fruit. Gently press the coconut to coat the fruit on all sides.

43

OTHER FRUIT POSSIBILITIES

cantaloupe	grapes	papaya
strawberries	nectarines	watermelon
pears	kiwi	peaches

Dumbo's Broccoli Slaw

Serves 4

UTENSILS

❖ Medium bowl

❖ 1 cup dry measuring cup

❖ 1 cup liquid measuring cup

❖ Mixing spoon

INGREDIENTS

❖ 2 cups broccoli slaw OR cabbage cole slaw (see Minnie Minder)

❖ 1/4 cup seasoned rice vinegar OR white vinegar with 1 tablespoon sugar added

❖ Salt and pepper to taste

Baloo says:

In the jungle we eat lots of fruits and veggies. They're colorful and delicious. Eat at least five servings of these crispy-crunchy, sweet-juicy treats every day. Need some ideas? Here are a few:

Whirl your favorite fruit (strawberries, peaches, kiwi) with low-fat yogurt or milk in a blender.

Stir fresh or frozen veggies—of all different colors—into rice, pasta, and soups at the end of the recipe. Cook a few minutes longer to be sure they're heated through.

Visit the salad bar in restaurants and supermarkets. Pick lots of different color vegetables to get the best variety.

Top pancakes (Mickey's favorite), waffles, toast, bagels, yogurt, or whole grain cereals with chopped or dried fruits.

Toss a can (or box) of 100% pure juice or a bag of cut up veggies or dried fruits into your backpack or gym bag for an easy snack.

Broccoli slaw and cabbage slaw are in the produce section of the supermarket. They are already preshredded and are packaged in plastic bags.

PLACE the broccoli slaw in a medium bowl.

ADD the vinegar. Mix well.

SEASON with salt and pepper to taste.

Thumper's Buttered Baby Carrots

Serves 4

UTENSILS

❖ 1-quart saucepan and cover

❖ 1 cup liquid measuring cup

❖ 1 knife

❖ 1 fork

❖ Kitchen scissors

❖ Toothpicks, if desired

INGREDIENTS

❖ One 16-ounce package peeled, ready-to-eat baby carrots

❖ 1/4 cup orange juice

❖ 1/4 cup water

❖ 2 tablespoons salted butter OR margarine

❖ 2 sprigs fresh dill OR parsley

❖ Salt to taste

Mickey's Nutri Tip

I bet everyone always tells you that carrots are good for your eyes. Guess what? They're right. It's because carrots have lots of vitamin A. Vitamin A keeps muscles strong, too. It even keeps gums and teeth healthy.

Look on the wrapper of the butter or margarine. You will see lines that show how much equals a tablespoon. Use a knife and press lightly on the paper at 2 tablespoons. Open the wrapper and cut the piece you need.

COMBINE the carrots, juice, water, and butter in a 1-quart saucepan.

(Ask an Adult) **COVER** the pan, and cook over medium-low heat for 10 to 15 minutes or until the carrots are tender. (Use a fork to test when they're done.)

UNCOVER the pan when the carrots are tender, and cook a few minutes longer, until most of the juice is gone.

(Ask an Adult) **USE** the kitchen scissors to snip the dill, or parsley, into the pan. Sprinkle with salt, if desired. Stir and serve. (It's fun to eat these carrots with toothpicks.)

47

Mushu says:

Snacks are smart. Between-meal treats are a good way to keep your energy going. Snacks fuel up your body like gas fuels up a car. To keep your engine running smoothly try some of these:

- *Rice crackers with PB & J*
- *Whole grain cereal (not just for breakfast!) with milk and fresh fruit or berries*
- *Giant fresh strawberries drizzled with a little chocolate syrup*
- *Air-popped popcorn sprinkled with parmesan cheese*
- *Banana slices covered with peanut butter and chopped dry-roasted peanuts*
- *Whole wheat pita triangles (one round bread cut in four pieces) topped with low-fat whipped cream cheese or peanut butter, or dunked in your favorite salsa or dip*
- *Frozen grapes (after you wash them, pat dry with a paper towel or clean kitchen towel. Remove the stems, then place the grapes in a single layer in a shallow pan, and place in the freezer.) A simple frosty treat!*

Alice's Cheesy Rice

Serves 4

UTENSILS

- ❖ 1 1/2-quart saucepan
- ❖ 1 cup liquid measuring cup
- ❖ 1 cup dry measuring cup
- ❖ Mixing spoon
- ❖ 1/2 cup dry measuring cup
- ❖ Oven mitts

INGREDIENTS

- ❖ 2 cups water
- ❖ 1 cup long-grain rice
- ❖ 3/4 cup shredded cheddar OR Monterey Jack cheese
- ❖ 1/2 cup reduced-fat sour cream

Mickey's Nutri Tip

Alice loves cheese because it tastes so good, and rice gives her lots of energy. When I make this I like to add some (thawed) frozen peas or cooked carrots when I stir in the cheese and sour cream. That makes it look pretty, and we get vegetables at the same time!

BRING the water to a boil over high heat in a 1 1/2-quart saucepan.

 STIR in the rice. Reduce heat to low. Cover and cook for about 20 minutes, or until most of the liquid is absorbed. Ask for help when checking the rice. Be sure to use oven mitts when taking the cover off the pot, and keep your face away when opening it (see Minnie Minder, page 41).

ADD the cheese and sour cream to the rice. Stir well until it is completely blended. Cover, and let stand for 1 minute so the cheese melts completely.

49

Nala says:

Protein makes me strong. You can be, too. Eat 2 to 3 servings each day. Just one chicken leg, a small burger, 1 egg, 1/2 cup cooked beans, or 1/3 cup of nuts is a serving. Make lean—less fat—choices for trim bodies.

Pocahontas's Triple Corn Bread

Makes one 9-inch square pan

UTENSILS

- ❖ One 9-inch square pan
- ❖ Strainer
- ❖ Small bowl
- ❖ Large mixing bowl
- ❖ Medium mixing spoon OR whisk
- ❖ Medium mixing bowl
- ❖ 1 cup dry measuring cup
- ❖ 1 teaspoon measuring spoon
- ❖ 1/2 teaspoon measuring spoon
- ❖ 1 cup liquid measuring cup
- ❖ 1 tablespoon measuring spoon
- ❖ Oven mitt
- ❖ Wire baking rack
- ❖ Cutting knife

INGREDIENTS

- ❖ Nonstick cooking spray
- ❖ One 7-ounce can Mexicorn niblets
- ❖ 1 cup yellow stone-ground cornmeal
- ❖ 1 cup all-purpose flour
- ❖ 2 teaspoons baking powder
- ❖ 1/2 teaspoon baking soda
- ❖ 1/2 teaspoon salt
- ❖ 1 egg
- ❖ 1 cup low-fat buttermilk OR plain yogurt
- ❖ 1/3 cup corn oil
- ❖ 2 tablespoons honey

PREHEAT oven to 425°F
(400°F if using a glass pan).

SPRAY the baking pan with nonstick
cooking spray. Set aside.

USE a strainer, with a small bowl underneath to
catch the liquid, to drain the corn. Set
aside the corn. Throw away the liquid.

COMBINE the cornmeal, flour, baking powder, baking soda,
and salt in a large bowl. Stir (or whisk) to mix it well.

USE the same spoon or whisk to combine the egg, buttermilk (OR
plain yogurt), oil, and honey in a medium bowl until it is blended.

POUR the egg mixture into the cornmeal mixture and stir just until it is
combined. (This is a dry, thick batter.) Stir in the corn. (Don't
overmix this batter. It needs just enough stirring to mix all the
ingredients together.)

SCRAPE the mixture into the prepared pan.
Lightly smooth the top to make an even layer.

BAKE for 20 minutes, or until golden brown, and the bread pulls away
from the sides of the pan.

Ask an Adult **REMOVE** the pan from the oven using oven mitt. Place the pan on a wire
rack to cool for about 10 minutes. Carefully cut the bread into
squares. This bread is very good served warm.

Minnie Minder

You can make a substitute for butter-milk or yogurt if you don't have any. In a 1 cup liquid measuring cup combine 1 tablespoon of lemon juice and just enough milk to make 1 cup. Let that stand for 10 minutes, then use as directed.

When measuring the honey, rub a little oil on the spoon first. Then the honey will slide right off the spoon, and into the bowl.

Dinner

- ❖ Lady's Favorite Pasta

- ❖ Tramp's Favorite Pasta

- ❖ Mulan's Fresh Fish Sticks

- ❖ Hercules' Powerhouse Meat Loaf

- ❖ Pluto's Power-Packed Pizza

- ❖ Mufasa's Mouthwatering Chops

Lady's Favorite Pasta

Serves 6 to 8

UTENSILS

- ❖ Small cutting knife
- ❖ Cutting board
- ❖ Can opener
- ❖ Medium microwave-safe bowl
- ❖ Plastic wrap
- ❖ Oven mitt
- ❖ 6-quart pot
- ❖ Large strainer OR colander
- ❖ Slotted spoon (a cooking spoon with holes)

INGREDIENTS

- ❖ 1 large garlic clove
- ❖ One 13 3/4-ounce can reduced-sodium chicken broth
- ❖ 2 tablespoons olive oil
- ❖ One 16-ounce package dried cappellini pasta
- ❖ 1 cup grated Parmesan cheese
- ❖ 1/2 cup fresh basil leaves OR parsley leaves

It's easy to forget that water can be heavy— especially big pots of it. Always ask for help when cooking pasta.

The piece of garlic that you buy in the store is called a bulb, or head, of garlic. Each one of the sections that can be separated is called a clove.

 PEEL the garlic, and cut it into 4 pieces.

OPEN the can of chicken broth and pour it into a medium microwave-safe bowl. Cover the bowl with plastic wrap. Microwave on HIGH for 3 minutes.

REMOVE the bowl from the microwave using the oven mitt. Carefully remove the plastic wrap (see Minnie Minder, page 41). Add the olive oil to the broth, and set aside.

 FILL a 6-quart pot with about 4 quarts of water. Bring to a boil over high heat.

ADD the pasta carefully. Stir. Cook the pasta for 10 to 12 minutes until tender, or according to the package directions.

 DRAIN the pasta over the sink using a large strainer, or colander. Then return the pasta to the pot.

REMOVE the garlic pieces from the broth mixture using the slotted spoon. Carefully pour the broth mixture, and half of the Parmesan cheese, over the pasta in the pot. Stir it well.

SERVE with the remaining Parmesan cheese sprinkled on top. You can also place a few fresh basil leaves OR parsley sprigs over each dish to make it look attractive.

55

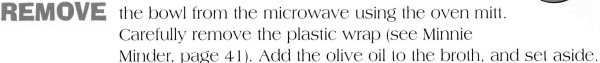

Pumbaa says:

Rice, noodles, tortillas, bread, oatmeal, spaghetti, couscous, pretzels, and cold cereal are the foods to eat the most of each day. Just one slice of bread, a half cup of cooked rice or macaroni, one tortilla, or 3/4 cup of cold cereal is a serving from this group. Add 'em up. Six isn't so much after all.

Tramp's Favorite Pasta

Serves 6 to 8

UTENSILS

- 6-quart pot
- 1-quart saucepan
- Can opener
- Large cooking spoon
- Large strainer OR colander

INGREDIENTS

- One 24-ounce jar mild salsa
- One 15-ounce can black beans, drained
- One 16-ounce package multicolored fusilli pasta
- 1 cup shredded low-fat Monterey Jack cheese OR shredded low-fat cheddar cheese
- 1 cup fresh cilantro OR coriander leaves
- 1 cup fat-free sour cream (if desired)

Mickey's Nutri Tip

Don't forget that beans are a great source of protein. Packed with fiber, they also count as a vegetable and come in lots of different colors and sizes. What a bonus!

Look in the dairy section for cheese that is already shredded to make this recipe easier. You can grate your own, but be careful of fingers and knuckles. No scrapes!

 BRING 4 quarts of water to a boil in a 6-quart pot.

POUR the jar of salsa into a 1-quart saucepan. Add the beans. Simmer on low heat for about 10 minutes, stirring occasionally.

 **ADD** the pasta carefully to the boiling water. Stir. Cook the pasta for 12 to 15 minutes, until tender, or according to package directions.

DRAIN the pasta over the sink using a large strainer, or colander. Then return the pasta to the pot.

ADD the salsa and beans to the pasta. Stir carefully.

SERVE the pasta with shredded cheese and cilantro OR coriander leaves sprinkled on top. (You might like to have some sour cream on the side, for dipping the pasta.)

57

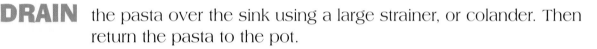

Mulan's Fresh Fish Sticks

Serves 4

UTENSILS

- ❖ Baking sheet
- ❖ Cutting board
- ❖ Kitchen scissors OR knife
- ❖ Medium bowl
- ❖ 1 tablespoon measuring spoon
- ❖ Plastic food storage bag
- ❖ Oven mitt

INGREDIENTS

- ❖ Nonstick cooking spray
- ❖ 1 pound flounder, catfish, OR white fish fillets
- ❖ 2 egg whites
- ❖ 2 tablespoons water
- ❖ 1 cup seasoned bread crumbs
- ❖ Tartar sauce (if desired)

PREHEAT the oven to 400°F. Spray a baking sheet with cooking spray. Set aside.

(Ask an Adult) **PLACE** the fish fillets on a cutting board. Carefully cut them into one-and-a-half-inch strips using kitchen scissors OR knife.

MIX the egg whites and water together in a medium bowl until blended.

POUR the bread crumbs into a plastic bag.

DIP each fish strip into the egg mixture. Then drop each piece into the plastic bag. Close the bag, or seal it with a tie. Shake the bag to coat all the fish strips with bread crumbs.

PLACE each coated strip on the baking sheet. Leave some space in between each one.

(Ask an Adult) **BAKE** for about 15 minutes, or until slightly browned and crisp.

(Ask an Adult) **REMOVE** the baking sheet from the oven, using oven mitt.

SERVE with tartar sauce, if desired.

Mickey's Nutri Tip

Your body needs different foods. Milk, yogurt, and cheese build strong bones. Fish, lean pork, chicken, and beans have protein for muscles. Carrots, broccoli, and sweet potatoes keep your eyes, skin, and hair healthy. For lasting energy eat rice, whole wheat English muffins, and whole grain cereals. In other words, eat a variety of foods every day.

Hercules' Powerhouse Meat Loaf

Serves 4 to 6

UTENSILS

- Potato peeler
- Cutting board
- Chopping knife
- Food processor
- 1 cup measuring cup
- 1/4 teaspoon measuring spoon
- 1/8 teaspoon measuring spoon
- 1 soup spoon
- Nonstick 12-muffin-cup pan OR 2 six-muffin-cup pans
- Oven mitt
- Meat thermometer
- 2 forks

INGREDIENTS

- 1 medium potato
- 1 small onion
- 1 medium tomato
- 1 stalk celery
- 10 peeled ready-to-eat baby carrots (OR 2 large carrots, washed and peeled)
- 1/2 pound lean ground beef
- 1 cup packaged bread crumbs
- 2 egg whites
- 1/4 teaspoon salt
- 1/8 teaspoon pepper
- Mustard and ketchup in squeezable bottles

PREHEAT oven to 325°F.

 PEEL the potato, using a potato peeler. Set aside.

 CUT a thin slice from each end of the onion.
Take off the outside skin. Set aside.

 **CHOP** each of the vegetables (potato, onion, tomato,
and celery) on the cutting board into 4 or 5 pieces.

PUT all the vegetables (including the baby carrots) into
the workbowl of a food processor.

ADD the meat, bread crumbs, egg whites, salt, and pepper.

PLACE the lid on the food processor, and lock it in place. Turn on
the processor. Let it run for about 1 to 2 minutes, until all the
vegetables are chopped and combined with the meat.

TURN OFF the food processor. Unplug the cord, and remove the lid.

FILL each of the muffin cups with the meat loaf mixture using
the soup spoon (see Minnie Minder).

DECORATE the top of each one with mustard and ketchup.

 PLACE the pan carefully in the oven using oven mitt. Bake for 45 minutes,
or until a meat thermometer placed in the center reads 160°F.

REMOVE the muffin pan carefully from the oven, using oven mitt.
Gently remove each meat loaf using one fork underneath
to lift it out, and another fork on top to hold it steady.

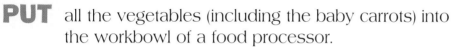

Minnie Minder

If your muffin pan is not a nonstick kind, spray each little cup with nonstick cooking spray first. That helps each meat loaf come out of the pan easily.

A meat thermometer is the BEST way to be sure meat is cooked right. That's important because sometimes bacteria in raw meat can make you sick.

61

Pluto's Power-Packed Pizza

Serves 4

UTENSILS

- Cutting board
- Slicing knife
- 2 nonstick baking sheets
- 1 cup measuring cup
- 1 tablespoon measuring spoon
- Large bowl
- 1 pizza cutter OR cutting knife
- Oven mitts

INGREDIENTS

- One 10-ounce package refrigerated pizza dough
- 1 medium tomato
- 1 small onion
- 1/2 cup prepared tomato sauce OR mild salsa
- 1 1/2 cups lettuce, torn into small pieces
- 8 small pitted black olives
- 2 ounces shredded pizza cheese (1/2 cup)
- 2 tablespoons prepared fat-free Italian dressing

FOR THE PIZZA CRUSTS

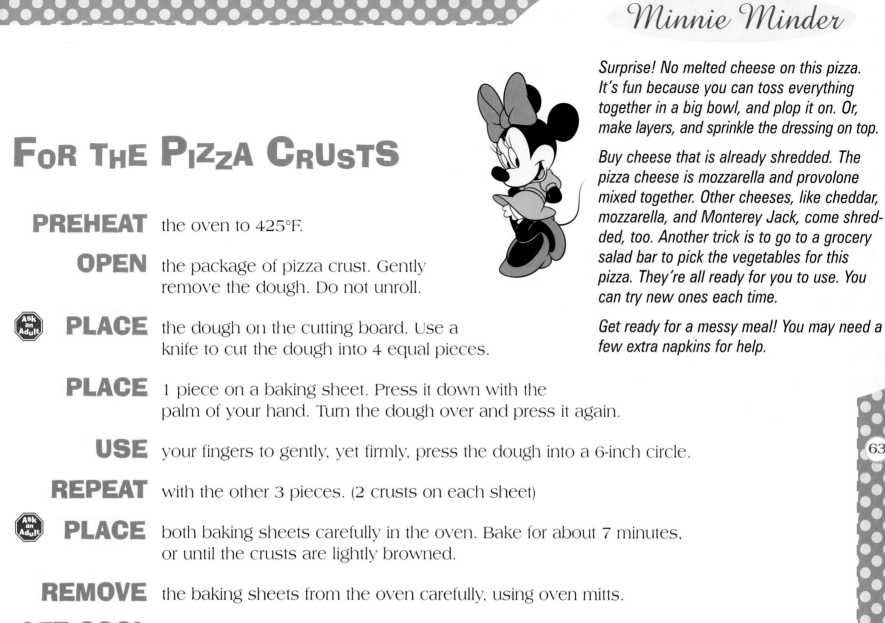

Surprise! No melted cheese on this pizza. It's fun because you can toss everything together in a big bowl, and plop it on. Or, make layers, and sprinkle the dressing on top.

Buy cheese that is already shredded. The pizza cheese is mozzarella and provolone mixed together. Other cheeses, like cheddar, mozzarella, and Monterey Jack, come shredded, too. Another trick is to go to a grocery salad bar to pick the vegetables for this pizza. They're all ready for you to use. You can try new ones each time.

Get ready for a messy meal! You may need a few extra napkins for help.

PREHEAT the oven to 425°F.

OPEN the package of pizza crust. Gently remove the dough. Do not unroll.

PLACE the dough on the cutting board. Use a knife to cut the dough into 4 equal pieces.

PLACE 1 piece on a baking sheet. Press it down with the palm of your hand. Turn the dough over and press it again.

USE your fingers to gently, yet firmly, press the dough into a 6-inch circle.

REPEAT with the other 3 pieces. (2 crusts on each sheet)

PLACE both baking sheets carefully in the oven. Bake for about 7 minutes, or until the crusts are lightly browned.

REMOVE the baking sheets from the oven carefully, using oven mitts.

LET COOL on the baking sheet for about 10 minutes, or until they are not too hot to touch. (If any of the crusts are puffed up press down lightly after they cool.)

(continued on next page)

63

Mickey's Nutri Tip

Pizza is a combination of almost all the food groups! You could also add sliced ham, or chicken, too. That would put in the protein, and give you all five groups.

(continued from previous page)

FOR THE PIZZA TOPPINGS

METHOD 1

PLACE the baked pizza shells on a cutting board or a kitchen counter. Place 2 tablespoons of the tomato sauce OR salsa over the top of each one. Use the back of the spoon to make a smooth, even layer of sauce. Set aside.

PEEL the onion. Cut it into thin slices or chop it into small pieces. Put it into a large bowl.

CUT the tomato into small pieces. Put it into the bowl.

ADD the rest of the ingredients to the bowl. Use your (clean!) hands to toss well.

PLACE 1/4 of the mixture on top of each pizza.

USE both your hands, and carefully place the finished pizza on a medium-size plate. Forget the knife and fork on this one. Have fun.

METHOD 2

PLACE the baked pizza shells on a cutting board or a kitchen counter. Place 2 tablespoons of the tomato sauce OR salsa over the top of each one. Use the back of the spoon to make a smooth, even layer of sauce. Set aside.

PEEL the onion. Cut it into thin slices or chop it into small pieces. Set aside.

CUT the tomato into thin slices or chop it into small pieces. Set aside.

PLACE a layer of each of the vegetables and the cheese evenly on each pizza. Sprinkle 1 tablespoon of the dressing over the top.

USE both your hands and carefully place the finished pizza on a medium-size plate. Forget the knife and fork on this one. Have fun.

Pongo says:

Know Your Nutrients! Just six simple things—nutrients—are found in foods. They're very important for growing up strong and healthy.

- **Protein** comes from lean pork, chicken, turkey, beef, beans, nuts, and eggs. Proteins help build, maintain, and repair the body.
- **Carbohydrates** fuel us up. Eat rice, crackers, tortillas, whole grain cereals, and breads, along with fruits and vegetables for lots of energy all day long.
- **Fats** provide lots of energy, too, and everyone's body needs a little. Use high-fat foods like mayonnaise, salad dressing, and whipped cream sparingly.
- **Vitamins and minerals** help get lots of things done for your body. They make strong bones and teeth, shiny hair, and smooth skin. Vitamins are named after letters of the alphabet, like A, C, D, and E. Calcium, iron, and potassium are some of the important minerals.
- **Water** is a nutrient, too. In fact, it's the most important one of all. And most of us don't drink enough water. Have at least four glasses each day. Try some when you're really feeling tired and see how good you feel. And, of course, *always* stop and take a sip whenever you see a water fountain.

Mufasa's Mouthwatering Chops

Serves 4

UTENSILS

- ❖ 1 large (12-inch) nonstick frying pan and cover
- ❖ 1 teaspoon measuring spoon
- ❖ Fork
- ❖ 1 cup liquid measuring cup
- ❖ Spatula

INGREDIENTS

- ❖ 4 boneless pork chops, each about 1-inch thick
- ❖ 1 teaspoon dried Italian seasoning
- ❖ 1/2 cup reduced-sodium chicken broth
- ❖ 1 tablespoon lemon juice
- ❖ Topper (see Mickey's Nutri Tip)

Mickey's Nutri Tip

Boneless pork chops have hardly any fat, and they're easy to eat. Here's how some of my pals like to top their chops. Have you got more ideas?

Jose's Mexican Fiesta
Mild salsa and grated Monterey Jack cheese.

Baloo's Bear Necessities
Canned (drained) pineapple slices with brown sugar.

Wendy's Honey of a Peach
Canned (drained) sliced peaches drizzled with honey.

Pinocchio's Honest-to-Goodness Favorite
Pizza sauce sprinkled with grated cheese.

The Beast's Feast
Mashed potatoes with grated cheddar cheese.

66

Pork is tender and juicy when you don't overcook it. These chops cook fast because there's no bone, and hardly any fat.

HEAT the frying pan over medium-high heat for 1 minute.

(Ask an Adult) **PLACE** the chops in the pan, carefully.

COOK for 2 minutes. Use a fork to turn the chops over. Cook 2 minutes longer.

SPRINKLE the Italian seasoning over the chops. Pour in the chicken broth, and lemon juice.

(Ask an Adult) **ADD** your favorite topper.

REDUCE heat to low. Cover, and cook for 2 minutes.

(Ask an Adult) **TRANSFER** the chops, using the spatula, to serving dishes.

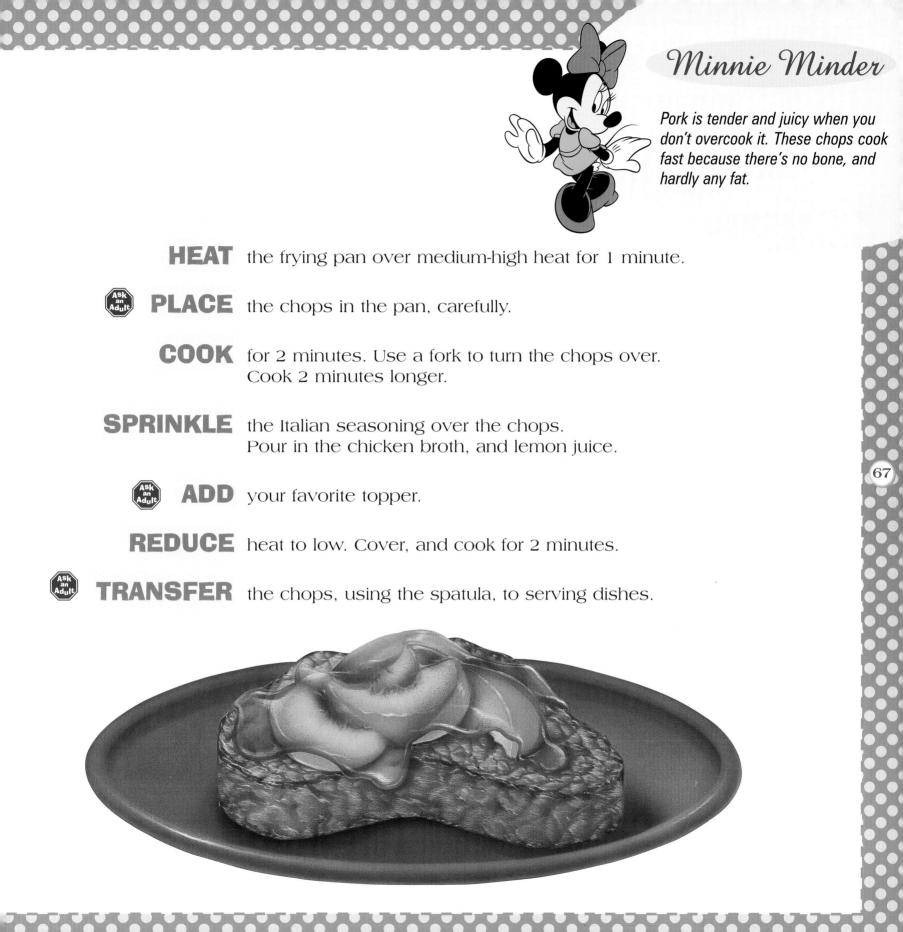

Beverages

❖ Mrs. Potts's Spiced Cider

❖ Peter Pan's Sparkling Pink Punch

❖ Jasmine's Fruitie Smoothie

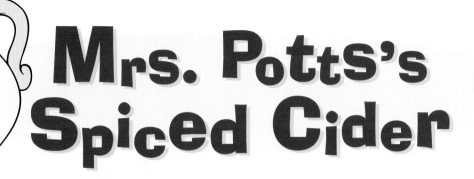

Mrs. Potts's Spiced Cider

Serves 2 (about 1 1/4 cups each)

UTENSILS

- 1 cup liquid measuring cup
- Small saucepan
- Oven mitt
- Slotted spoon
- 2 mugs

INGREDIENTS

- 1/2 cup orange juice
- 1 cinnamon stick, about 2-inches long
- 2 whole cloves
- 2 cups apple cider OR apple juice

COMBINE the orange juice, cinnamon stick, and cloves in the saucepan.

 BRING to a boil over high heat. Reduce heat to low, and simmer for 10 minutes.

 ADD the cider (or juice). Cook over high heat for 1 minute. Using an oven mitt, carefully remove the pan from the heat.

REMOVE the cinnamon stick and cloves using a slotted spoon.

 POUR the cider carefully into two mugs.

71

Mickey's Nutri Tip

When it's chilly outside, this keeps me warm inside. Mrs. P's juice combo is a vitamin C special.

Peter Pan's Sparkling Pink Punch

Serves 6 (about 1 cup each)

UTENSILS

- ❖ Can opener
- ❖ Large pitcher OR
  punch bowl and ladle
- ❖ Mixing spoon
- ❖ Plastic wrap
- ❖ Punch cups OR glasses

INGREDIENTS

- ❖ 2 1/2 cups unsweetened pineapple juice
- ❖ 2 cups pink grapefruit juice
- ❖ 1 1/2 cups water or
  sparkling water, chilled
- ❖ Grenadine syrup to taste (if desired)
- ❖ Fruit slices for garnish: orange slices,
  pineapple slices, kiwi slices, or whole
  strawberries (if desired)

Minnie Minder

Grenadine syrup is a deep red syrup that's used to color and flavor drinks. It is very sweet. Add a tablespoon, then taste the punch. If you need more, add another teaspoon.

This punch is not too fizzy. You can use water instead of the sparkling water if you want a bubble-free punch.

OPEN the cans of pineapple and grapefruit juice.

POUR the pineapple and grapefruit juices into a large pitcher. Stir.

COVER with plastic wrap and refrigerate until chilled.

STIR in the water OR sparkling water and some grenadine, if desired. Pour, or ladle, the punch into glasses.

GARNISH with a slice of fruit, if desired.

100% pure is what I look for when choosing juice. That means no added sugar or water. I like my vitamins and minerals straight from the source. You can use your favorite blend of juices. Just make sure they're pure.

Jasmine's Fruitie Smoothie

Serves 4 (about 1 cup each)

UTENSILS

* ❖ Blender OR food processor
* ❖ 1 cup liquid measuring cup
* ❖ 1/4 teaspoon measuring spoon (optional)
* ❖ 4 medium glasses

INGREDIENTS

* ❖ 1 medium, very ripe banana, peeled
* ❖ 1 cup fresh strawberries
* ❖ 1 cup nonfat plain yogurt OR low-fat milk
* ❖ 1/4 teaspoon vanilla (optional)
* ❖ 2 ice cubes

Oliver says:

Dairy foods are the best source of calcium. That means strong bones, teeth, and muscles. One cup of milk or yogurt, 1 ounce of cheese, 1 1/3 cups of cottage cheese, or 1 cup of frozen yogurt equal a serving. Have 3 to 4 servings each day. Pick some low-fat or fat-free foods here whenever you can.

BREAK the banana into 3 or 4 pieces, and place in a blender container OR the workbowl of a food processor.

RINSE the strawberries, and pull off the stems. Put them in the container.

ADD the rest of the ingredients. Put the lid of the blender tightly in place.

BLEND for about 30 seconds, or until smooth and creamy.

POUR into glasses and serve.

Mickey's Nutri Tip

I like to have this for a quick snack, or a good, fast breakfast. It's got calcium, vitamins A and C, and lots of fiber. Try other fruits like kiwi, pineapple, melon, or peaches for a new taste each time.

Desserts

- ❖ Chip 'n' Dale's Chocolate Peanut Clusters

- ❖ King Louie's Banana Boat

- ❖ Pinocchio's Pear Sundae

- ❖ 101 Dalmatians' Brownies

- ❖ Happy's Crunchy Rice Squares

- ❖ Snow White's Applesauce Cookie Bars

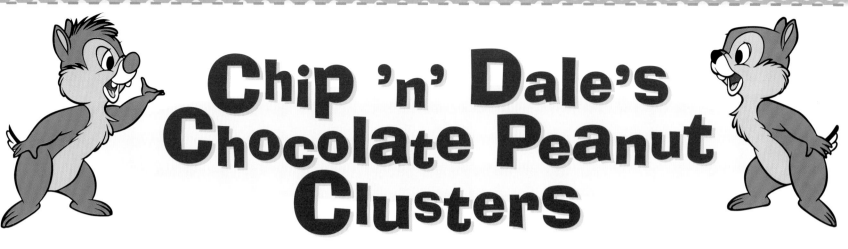

Chip 'n' Dale's Chocolate Peanut Clusters

Makes about 20 pieces

UTENSILS

- ❖ Medium microwave-safe bowl
- ❖ 1 cup dry measuring cup
- ❖ Oven mitt
- ❖ 1/2 cup dry measuring cup
- ❖ 1 mixing spoon
- ❖ 1 teaspoon measuring spoon
- ❖ 2 dinner plates

INGREDIENTS

- ❖ 1 cup reduced-fat semisweet chocolate chips
- ❖ 1/2 cup unsalted dry roasted peanuts
- ❖ 1/2 cup light OR dark raisins

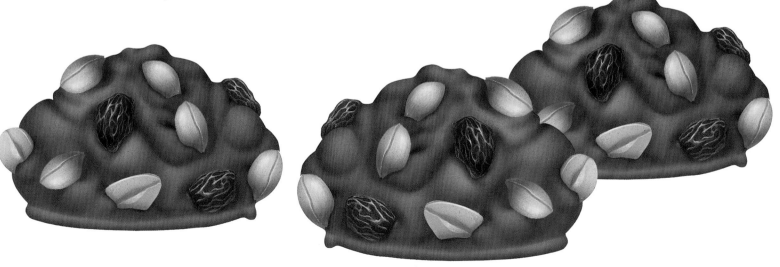

Ariel says:

There are no good foods or bad foods. Some foods you definitely want to eat more of than others. Eat plenty of beans, corn, apples, bananas, rice, lean meats and low-fat milk each day. Then sometimes you can have cake, chips, and candy, too.

POUR the chocolate chips into a microwave-safe bowl.

MICROWAVE on HIGH for 2 to 2 1/2 minutes, or until almost melted.

REMOVE the bowl from the microwave using an oven mitt.

ADD the peanuts and raisins to the chocolate and stir well.

DROP the mixture by teaspoonsful onto the plates.

REFRIGERATE for about 15 minutes, or until the clusters harden. Gently twist to remove from plates.

Mickey's Nutri Tip

Peanuts and raisins are both high in fiber and carbohydrates. That makes them a high-energy food. Did you know that peanuts are also a good source of protein?

King Louie's Banana Boat

Serves 1

UTENSILS

❖ Toaster oven

❖ Cutting board

❖ Knife

❖ 8-inch piece of aluminum foil

❖ 1 tablespoon measuring spoon

❖ Oven mitt

INGREDIENTS

❖ 1 medium banana, peeled

❖ 1 tablespoon chocolate chips

❖ 1 tablespoon miniature marshmallows

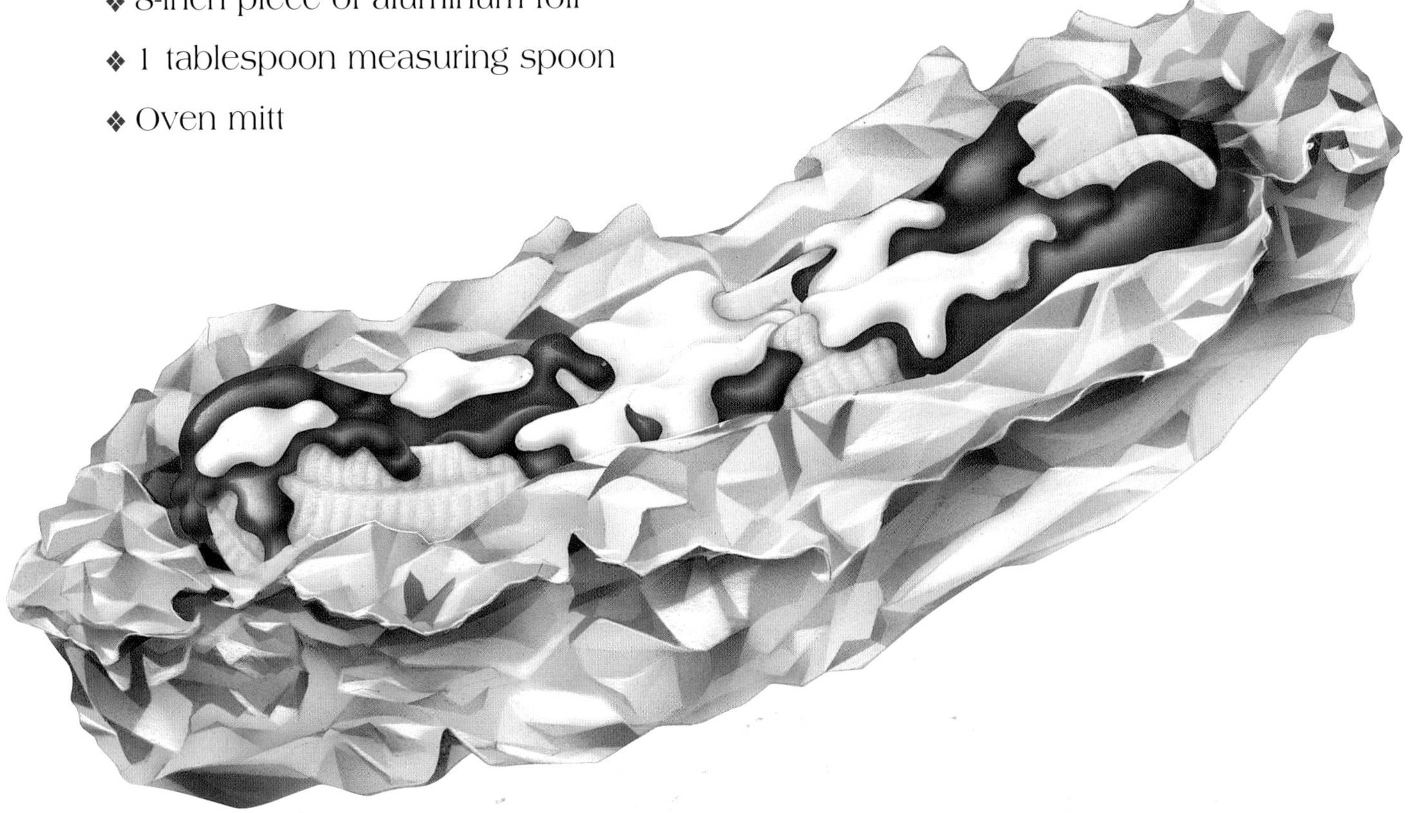

PREHEAT a toaster oven (or regular oven) to 400°F.

 **PLACE** the banana on a cutting board, and cut it in half, making 2 long pieces.

PLACE the pieces side by side on the aluminum foil.

SPRINKLE the chocolate chips and marshmallows on top of the banana.

BRING up the sides of the foil to cover the banana and crimp, making a sealed package.

PLACE the banana package in the middle of the oven (directly on the rack), and bake for 15 to 20 minutes, until the chocolate chips and marshmallows are melted.

REMOVE the packet from oven using an oven mitt. Wait 1 minute for it to cool a bit.

UNFOLD the foil carefully. Fold down the sides to make a small boat.
King Louie's banana boat may be served right in the foil boat.

Mickey's Nutri Tip

This ape is no dummy. He knows how to take a little chocolate and make it a healthy snack. Do you think he knows bananas are a high-energy food? They are also a good source of potassium and carbohydrates.

Pinocchio's Pear Sundae

Serves 4

UTENSILS

❖ Can opener

❖ Medium strainer

❖ 2 medium bowls

❖ 4 dessert (small) plates

❖ Ice cream scoop

❖ 1 teaspoon measuring spoon

INGREDIENTS

❖ One 15-ounce can pear slices, packed in juice

❖ 4 sponge cake dessert shells*

❖ 2 cups low-fat frozen yogurt (your favorite flavor)

❖ 8 teaspoons chocolate syrup

*Look for the dessert shells in the deli or produce section of the supermarket. They are always available when fresh strawberries are in season. Otherwise, use slices of low-fat pound cake, or toasted whole wheat waffles.

Place the pears in the refrigerator to get them nice and cold before you make this recipe. Try canned sliced peaches, cherries, or other fruit, too!

OPEN the can of pears.

DRAIN the juice from the pears using a strainer, with a medium bowl underneath (to catch the juice).

PLACE one dessert shell on each plate. Place one scoop (about 1/2 cup) of yogurt on top.

ARRANGE about 4 pear slices (or enough to use all the pears) around the edge of each dessert.

DRIZZLE two teaspoons of the chocolate syrup over each plate of yogurt and pears, and serve.

83

101 Dalmatians' Brownies

Makes 12 to 16 brownies

UTENSILS

❖ 8-inch square baking pan

❖ 2 medium mixing bowls

❖ Electric mixer

❖ 1/2 cup dry measuring cup

❖ 1 cup liquid measuring cup

❖ 1/3 cup dry measuring cup

❖ 1/4 cup measuring cup

❖ 1 teaspoon measuring spoon

❖ 1/2 teaspoon measuring spoon

❖ 1 tablespoon measuring spoon

❖ Mixing spoon

❖ Oven mitt

INGREDIENTS

❖ Nonstick cooking spray

❖ 1/2 cup sugar

❖ 1/3 cup vegetable oil

❖ 1/3 cup light corn syrup

❖ 1 teaspoon vanilla extract

❖ 2 egg whites

❖ 2/3 cup all-purpose flour

❖ 1/2 teaspoon baking powder

❖ 1/2 teaspoon salt

❖ 2 tablespoons unsweetened cocoa powder

PREHEAT the oven to 325°F (300°F if using glass). Lightly spray the baking pan with non-stick cooking spray. Set aside.

COMBINE the sugar, oil, corn syrup, vanilla, and egg whites in a mixing bowl. Beat on low speed for 1 to 2 minutes until well blended. Turn off mixer.

ADD the flour, baking powder, and salt. Beat again on low speed until just blended.

REMOVE 1/2 cup of the mixture. Put it into the other mixing bowl. Add the cocoa, and stir until blended.

POUR the white batter into the prepared baking pan. Spread with the back of a spoon to cover the bottom of the pan.

DROP the chocolate batter on top of the white batter using a teaspoon to make lots of spots. (Use your clean finger to push it off the spoon!)

Ask an Adult **BAKE** for 25 minutes, or until the brownies feel firm to the touch.

Ask an Adult **REMOVE** from the oven, using oven mitt. Let cool, and cut into squares.

85

Minnie Minder

The only way to know the real temperature inside the oven is to use a special oven thermometer. Yes! Sometimes the numbers on the dial are wrong. Hang the thermometer in a cold oven, close to where you'll place the pan. Turn the oven on and give it about 10 minutes to come up to where you set it. Adjust if necessary.

Happy's Crunchy Rice Squares

Makes 24 squares

UTENSILS

- ❖ 13 x 9-inch baking pan
- ❖ Large mixing bowl
- ❖ 1 cup dry measuring cup
- ❖ 1/2 cup dry measuring cup
- ❖ Large mixing spoon
- ❖ Large microwave-safe bowl
- ❖ 1 tablespoon measuring spoon
- ❖ Oven mitt
- ❖ Knife

INGREDIENTS

- ❖ Nonstick cooking spray
- ❖ 5 1/2 cups crisp rice cereal
- ❖ One 6-ounce package dried chopped mixed fruits (about 1 cup)
- ❖ 1/4 cup toasted wheat germ
- ❖ 1 teaspoon ground cinnamon
- ❖ One 10-ounce bag large marshmallows
- ❖ 2 tablespoons vegetable oil
- ❖ 2 tablespoons low-fat milk

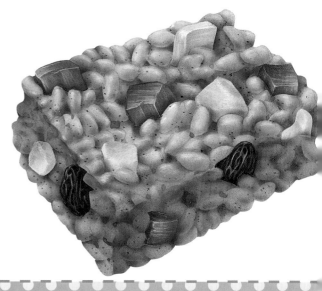

Minnie Minder

Use a 12 1/4 x 8 1/4-inch foil pan if you are making these snacks for school or a party. The (disposable but recyclable) pan makes it easy to take them anywhere.

SPRAY the baking pan with nonstick cooking spray. Set aside.

COMBINE the cereal, dried fruit, wheat germ, and cinnamon in a large mixing bowl. Set aside.

COMBINE the marshmallows, oil, and milk in a large microwave-safe bowl. Microwave, uncovered, on HIGH for 1 minute. Stir the mixture. Microwave again, on HIGH, for 1 minute, or until the mixture is completely smooth.

REMOVE the bowl from the microwave, using the oven mitt. Pour the marshmallow mixture over the cereal. Stir to mix well. This gets thick, so you may need help here. (Some of the wheat germ may still be left in the bowl. Just stir in as much as you can.)

SPREAD the mixture into the baking pan using a large mixing spoon, and make an even layer. (You can also spray some cooking oil on your fingers— washed, please—to pat the mixture into the pan.)

 PUT the pan into the refrigerator and chill until just firm. Cut into squares.

Snow White's Applesauce Cookie Bars

Makes 24 bars

UTENSILS

- 13 x 9-inch baking pan
- Large mixing bowl
- 1 cup dry measuring cup
- 1/2 cup dry measuring cup
- 1 teaspoon measuring spoon
- 1/4 teaspoon measuring spoon
- Whisk
- Medium mixing bowl
- 1 cup liquid measuring cup
- Electric mixer
- Rubber scraper OR spoon
- Oven mitt
- Toothpick OR cake tester
- Wire cooling rack
- Knife

INGREDIENTS

- Nonstick cooking spray
- 1 1/4 cups all-purpose flour
- 1/2 cup whole wheat flour
- 2 teaspoons ground cinnamon
- 1 teaspoon baking powder
- 1/4 teaspoon ground nutmeg
- 1/4 teaspoon salt
- 1 cup unsweetened applesauce*
- 1/3 cup vegetable oil
- 1 cup packed light brown sugar
- 1 cup dark raisins

*If sweetened applesauce is all you have, use the same amount but reduce the light brown sugar to 3/4 cup.

PREHEAT oven to 350°F. Spray the baking pan with nonstick cooking spray. Set aside.

You can also use a 12 1/4 x 8 1/4-inch foil pan for this recipe (like Happy's Crunchy Rice Squares, page 86). It's an easy way to take these bars to a party, or to school. Don't forget to recycle!

WHISK or stir together the two flours, cinnamon, baking powder, nutmeg, and salt in a large bowl.

COMBINE the applesauce, oil, brown sugar, and raisins in a medium bowl. Use an electric mixer, on low speed, and beat for 1 minute, or until the brown sugar is dissolved.

POUR the applesauce mixture into the flour mixture. Stir in the raisins. Beat again on low speed, just until blended.

SCRAPE the batter into the pan, using a rubber scraper or spoon. Spread to make even layer.

(Ask an Adult) **PLACE** the pan in the oven, using oven mitt. Bake for about 25 minutes. Use a toothpick (or cake tester) to poke the middle of the pan. If it comes out dry, the bars are done. If not, bake a few minutes longer.

(Ask an Adult) **TAKE** the pan out of the oven, using oven mitt. Place it on a wire rack to cool. Cut into squares.

89

Putting It All Together

Here are some ways for you to take some of the recipes and combine them into a meal or a snack.

HOLIDAY BREAKFAST

Pineapple or Cranberry Juice Cocktail
Mickey's Whole Wheat Honey Pancakes (page 20)
Sliced Banana
Low-Fat Milk

EVERYDAY BREAKFAST

Orange Juice
Goofy's Smart-Start Oatmeal (page 16)
Low-Fat Milk

INVITE A FRIEND FOR LUNCH

Goofy's Easy as A-B-C Vegetable Soup (page 30)
Whole Wheat Roll
Peter Pan's Sparkling Pink Punch (page 72)
Graham Crackers

WHAT'S FOR DINNER?

Tossed Salad with Low-Fat Dressing
Tramp's Favorite Pasta (page 56)
Italian Bread

Tossed Salad

Use a big bowl and make sure all the veggies are washed and dried before you use them. Use several of the items below each time you make a salad. Once you have the veggies in the bowl, add a few tablespoons of low-fat dressing or sprinkle a little oil and vinegar on top. Then toss well, using two large spoons or salad tongs. (To toss a salad means gently combine all the ingredients within the bowl. No veggies in the air, please!)

- *romaine lettuce*
- *iceberg lettuce*
- *cherry tomatoes*
- *cucumber slices*
- *mushroom slices*

- *radish slices*
- *avocado cubes*
- *red or green pepper strips*
- *red or white canned beans (drained)*

WEEKEND DINNER

Tomato Juice Appetizer
Mufasa's Mouthwatering Chops (page 66)
Thumper's Buttered Baby Carrots (page 46)
Baked Red Potatoes
Frozen Yogurt

Preheat oven to 350 °F. Scrub four medium-size potatoes, and pat dry with a paper towel. Pierce the pototoes a few times with a fork. Bake for about 45 minutes, or until tender.

AFTER SCHOOL SNACKS

Drink a glass of low-fat milk or chocolate milk with any one of these fun treats:

Aladdin's Magic Carpet Rolls (page 26)
Rafiki's Coconut Fruit Kabobs (page 42)
Happy's Crunchy Rice Squares (page 86)
Abu's Baked Apples (page 40)

WE'RE HAVING A DINNER PARTY

The Sultan's Hummus Dip with Veggies (page 38)
Hercules' Powerhouse Meatloaf (page 60)
Peas and Carrots
Alice's Cheesy Rice (page 48)
Pinocchio's Pear Sundae (page 82)
Mrs. Potts's Spiced Cider (page 70)

The Perfect Setting

A table that's pretty and clean makes the food taste extra good!

SETTING THE TABLE

❖ Dust or wipe the table with a damp—
  not wet—sponge.
❖ Use a tablecloth to cover the table or placemats
  for each person.
❖ Place a plate or bowl for each person about 1 inch
  from the edge of the table.
❖ Place a knife by the right side of the plate.
  Turn the blade of the knife toward the plate.
❖ Place a spoon next to the knife.

❖ Place a folded napkin on the left side of the plate.
❖ Place the fork by the left side of the plate (on top of
  the napkin, if you're not using napkin rings) with the
  tines (the part that holds the food) facing up.
❖ Place the beverage glass on the right, just above the
  tip of the knife.
❖ Place the salad plate or bowl (if you are having one)
  on the left above the fork.

CENTERPIECES

It's nice to have a centerpiece—a pretty arrangement in the middle of the table—especially for parties or special occasions. You can make your own centerpiece with lots of items found around the house or yard—the key is to be creative and have fun! Try fresh flowers in a vase, or make cut-out flowers from colored paper attached to stems made of pipe cleaners or sticks. For a theme, use holiday ornaments or even a favorite toy collection of bears or dolls. A bowl of fresh fruit, pine cones, or even colored balls, look terrific, too. Check out your library for books on creating imaginative and colorful centerpieces for every occasion. There are only two rules: Leave room for the plates and food! And don't create anything so high that you can't see your friends and family across the table!

NAPKINS

Everyone needs to stay tidy at the table, so napkins are a must! Whether paper or cloth, napkins can help adorn a table before they are placed in your lap. Here are some easy and fun ways to use napkins while setting the table.

❖ *Fold a napkin into a triangle and place beneath the fork.*

❖ *Use napkin rings—store-bought ones come in a variety of shapes, colors, and themes. Or you can make your own! Have an adult help you cut a paper towel roll into 1 1/2 inch strips (be careful not to crush the roll). Paint each strip with zany*

designs, or glue on macaroni in different shapes, or add glitter. You can also cover the strips with colored paper or felt. Each place at the table can have a different design. Mix and match, use your imagination. Once the rings are done (and make sure they're dry), roll the napkins up and poke through the rings. Place them at the top of the plate or directly on it.

❖ *Fold or roll the napkin so that it is an inch or so wide, then wrap it around the middle with different colored yarns or ribbons, or tie it with a bow. Center on the plate.*

Index

To Marlene and Jerry, Danielle and Rachael;
with much love and many thanks.

First Disney Press Paperback Edition 1999
Recipes © 1998 by Pat Baird.
Recipe Titles © 1998 Disney Enterprises, Inc.
Additional Texts © 1998 Disney Enterprises, Inc.
Artwork © 1998 Disney Enterprises, Inc.
Compilation © 1998 Disney Enterprises, Inc.

Printed in Singapore.

First Edition
1 3 5 7 9 10 8 6 4 2

Designed by Atif Toor.
Food Illustrations by Cindy Sass.

Library of Congress Catalog Card Number: 97-80313
ISBN: 0-7868-3230-4 (paperback)

For more Disney Press fun, visit www.disneybooks.com